Original title:
Lace Across the Mind

Copyright © 2025 Creative Arts Management OÜ
All rights reserved.

Author: Derek Caldwell
ISBN HARDBACK: 978-1-80586-059-4
ISBN PAPERBACK: 978-1-80586-531-5

Weaving Webs of Perception

In a twirl of thoughts so bright,
Silly notions take their flight.
Like a cat with yarn to chase,
We giggle at this tangled space.

Colors clash in jumbled cheer,
Thoughts like confetti, oh so near.
A circus dance upon the page,
Each quirkiness a little sage.

Knots of worry start to weave,
But laughter's thread we gladly cleave.
With every ponder, every jest,
We find play's joy and feel so blessed.

In this tapestry of jest,
Every twist can be a quest.
Wrap your mind in fun and glee,
And let bright whimsy set you free.

Ties to Thought

A jumbled knot of silly dreams,
Tangled threads burst at the seams.
Ideas dance with a goofy flair,
Whirling thoughts float in the air.

Mismatched socks in a dizzy spin,
Chasing laughter, let the fun begin.
Each whimsy twists with comic grace,
In mental knots, we find our place.

A Woven Journey

Through giggles spun like candy floss,
My thoughts embark, not at a loss.
They hop and skip, a joyful flight,
With paths that twist, it feels so right.

Like spaghetti on a dinner plate,
My brain's a mess, but isn't it great?
Every thought is a noodle, you see,
Tangled and wild, just let them be.

Patterns in the Ether

In clouds of cotton, where thoughts can roam,
Ideas like squirrels search for a home.
With every leap, a giggle burst,
In the playground of mind, we quench our thirst.

Patterns form and patterns fade,
Like shadows play in a grand charade.
Each wacky notion is a playful sign,
In this whimsical space, all is fine.

The Veils of Imagination

Curtains flutter in the calm of thought,
Behind them, mischief is expertly wrought.
A parade of quirks in a vivid hue,
Where whimsy runs wild, just for you.

Unruly squiggles spin and whirl,
In a carnival of dreams, we twirl.
With each small giggle, the veil comes apart,
Revealing the joys that burst from the heart.

Echoes in the Weave

In the garden of thoughts, I trip and I fall,
Tangled in memories, laughing through it all.
A sock puppet sitting, giving me advice,
Chasing after giggles—oh, isn't life nice?

Thoughts spinning like tops, in a colorful race,
A banana in pajamas had taken my place.
Questions swirl like confetti in the bright sun,
As I search for the punchline; oh, where is the fun?

Ribbons of Reminiscence

I found a lost ribbon beneath my old bed,
It whispered sweet secrets of things left unsaid.
Wrapped around memories, dusty but bold,
Telling me stories of adventures retold.

Jellybeans dancing in my cereal bowl,
Each bite a reminder of the candy we stole.
Nostalgia's a prankster, with slippery shoes,
It makes me believe that I'll never lose.

Tendrils of Insight

Tentacles tickling the back of my brain,
Whimsical whispers, driving me insane.
A cactus in slippers, so fuzzy and bright,
Offering wisdom late into the night.

Thoughts unravel like yarn from a careless cat,
Spinning yarns of nonsense; oh, imagine that!
Rubber chickens chat, as the clock strikes a tune,
In this mind-weaving circus, I'm howling at the moon.

The Veil of Understanding

Behind a curtain of giggles, I peek and I spy,
A garden of wonders that twinkle nearby.
A gnome wearing glasses, reading the news,
Spouting off trivia in his mismatched shoes.

Chasing my thoughts like a butterfly fleet,
While eating the gelato that drips down my feet.
Lessons learned lightly, with a wink and a grin,
In the dance of the silly, it's where I begin.

Delicate Veils of Thought

Whispers dance on fleeting air,
Bright ideas float without a care.
Tickle my brain with tales so spry,
Where giggles bloom, and thoughts can fly.

A tangled web of jests and glee,
Puns and quirks, all part of me.
Like butterflies in silly hats,
They flutter by, like playful cats.

An Interlaced Dreamscape

In a world where giggles sprout,
Silly socks don't see much doubt.
My pillow fights with dreams at night,
While unicorns take off in flight.

Laughter mingles with the stars,
As jellybeans ride in toy cars.
Thoughts wrapped up in candy floss,
In this land where logic's lost.

Fragments of Fabrication

Oddball notions weave and twine,
Like spaghetti on a dining line.
Bouncing thoughts like rubber balls,
With every twist, a giggle calls.

Socks that rhyme and hats that glow,
Silly dances, come join the show!
My mind's a patchwork, bright and loud,
Woven dreams that make me proud.

Chasing the Mental Tapestry

Nonsense trails through thick and thin,
With playful prompts that make me grin.
Chasing thoughts like butterflies,
They tickle me, oh what a surprise!

Patterns of laughter softly spin,
A jester's face, my closest kin.
In this chase, I'm never meek,
For silly thoughts are what I seek.

Constellations of Concepts

Thoughts float like stars,
Twinkling in the night,
Ideas collide and spark,
Creating cosmic delight.

In this galaxy of jest,
Comets zoom and trace,
Jokes orbit around,
In a heavenly embrace.

Nebulas of nonsense swirl,
In a dance of desire,
Every chuckle and giggle,
Ignites the cosmic fire.

So gather your wonders,
Let your dreams take a ride,
For in this vast expanse,
Humor is our guide.

Finespun Reflections

Threads of thought unwind,
In a tapestry so bright,
Each stitch a joke or pun,
Woven with pure delight.

Mirrors twist and bend,
Showing laughter's face,
Every glance reveals gold,
In this whimsical space.

Witty bursts of color,
Draped over the mundane,
Weaving joy's reflection,
In a fabric of refrain.

So let us spin our tales,
With yarns both bold and fine,
For in this silken dance,
Laughter's always mine.

Weaving the Ethereal

Threads of whimsy spin,
In a loom made of dreams,
Each strand a playful thought,
In a tapestry of schemes.

Woven fine and freckled,
Patterns shift and fly,
Join this comic quilting,
In the blink of an eye.

With every silly loop,
A chuckle finds its way,
Creating smiles in colors,
That brighten up the day.

So gather up your fabric,
Let your spirit unwind,
For in this art of fun,
Joy is all we'll find.

Echoes in Thread

Listen to the whispers,
In each woven strand,
Laughter softly echoes,
In the fabric of our land.

Tales bounce like rubber balls,
In a patchwork of delight,
Where every jibe and jab,
Makes the evening bright.

Stitches sing of antics,
In a chorus of jest,
Each loop a merry dance,
In this silly fest.

So weave your tales with glee,
Let your humor be heard,
For in this grand design,
Laughter is the word.

The Web of Introspection

In the corner, thoughts spin round,
Like lazy cats falling down.
Tangled ideas with a dash,
Oh, look! There goes my stash.

I searched for wisdom in my sock,
Found only crumbs and a tiny clock.
The brain's a maze, or so they say,
I need a map, or maybe just a tray.

I ponder deep while pouring tea,
Why is there no sense of glee?
A light bulb flickers, then goes dim,
I'm quite convinced it's all a whim.

With every twist, I start to see,
My thoughts prefer a life of spree.
So here's a toast to tangled threads,
And all the giggles in our heads.

Threads of the Infinite

Threads are dancing in my brain,
Their rhythm's like a runaway train.
They twist and turn, a playful guise,
Where logic sleeps and chaos flies.

I pulled one strand, it stretched so far,
It led me to a candy jar.
A marshmallow cloud, what a surprise,
Found there a stash of gummy fries!

In each new loop, I lose my way,
Should I dive in or just delay?
But laughter rings, my heart takes flight,
When nonsense brings pure delight.

Oh, tangled fibers of my fate,
You're in a mood to celebrate!
Let's weave a world of silly schemes,
Where every thought's a set of dreams.

Embroidered Epiphanies

I had a thought, it wore a gown,
With patterns bold and in renown.
But then it danced and slipped away,
    Inviting me for a wacky play.

Epiphanies in clashing hues,
Wiggling about in ratty shoes.
What's that? Oh, just my breakfast toast,
The only thing I'm fond of most!

Each stitch a giggle, every seam,
A wild ride through a silly dream.
With every thread I try to pin,
My brain declares, "Let's laugh and spin!"

So here I sit, with needle proud,
Embroidering thoughts into a cloud.
A tapestry of jests and cheer,
For life is better when we're near.

The Loom of Memories

At the loom of silly days,
I weave my thoughts in funny ways.
Each memory a wobbly stitch,
A dance of fools, a joyful glitch.

Remember when we chased the cat?
With bubble wrap and a loud spat?
Oh, what a mess, but what a thrill!
Those moments give my heart a chill.

Old yarns tangled in a heap,
As laughter echoes, not a peep.
Each thread a quirk, it pulls me tight,
I'm crafting joy from day to night.

So let's entwine our tales with glee,
A patchwork of our history.
For in this loom, where dreams unwind,
We find the fun we left behind.

Twisted Reflections

In a mirror, I see a grin,
But also a cat wearing thin.
My hair's a mess, who knew today,
That chaos could lead to such play?

Teapots giggle, cups do dance,
In this odd and silly trance.
A rubber chicken joins the show,
As laughter ebbs and flows.

Shadows of a Faded Memory

A memory of past delight,
Where squirrels wore hats, oh what a sight!
They argued about the best nut's taste,
While I, confused, just made haste.

Umbrellas danced in puddles wide,
While I pretended I could glide.
With every step, a shoe would squeak,
Echoing fun, just like a cheek.

The Net of the Unconscious

A web of dreams spun tight and fast,
Catching thoughts that never last.
I found a fish that claimed to sing,
A marvelous and monstrous thing!

It swam through circles, spun with glee,
While polka dots would dance with me.
A peanut took a stroll, so proud,
In my mind's circus, quite loud.

Stitches of Silence

In a quilt of quiet thoughts,
The rabbits plot their silly plots.
With threads of giggles, seams of cheer,
They stitch up smiles, never fear.

A whisper here, a chuckle there,
As donuts bounce without a care.
In every corner, joy unwinds,
Sewing up laughter, hearts and minds.

The Art of Mental Stitching

In a tapestry of ideas, I weave,
Threads of whimsy, I can't believe.
Crooked thoughts and tangled schemes,
Stitching laughter into wild dreams.

With needle sharp and colors bright,
I patch the chaos, quite a sight.
A little poke, a little prode,
What's life without a funny code?

Each thought a fabric, a quirky square,
Stitched together with the greatest care.
I hold the shears and snip away,
At silly notions made for play.

So let's embrace the crazy spin,
In this wild fabric, let's dive in.
For every knot and every twist,
Brings a giggle, you can't resist!

Warp and Weft of Wonder

Threads of whimsy dance and play,
In the loom where thoughts stray.
Warped ideas, soft and light,
Weaving laughter into the night.

With every shout of 'what the heck',
I spin around, a mental speck.
Tangled yarn makes for fun days,
In this fabric, silliness stays.

A jumpy thread, a wobbling weave,
What comes next, who could conceive?
Life's such a riot, a wiggly thread,
Stitched with humor and a bit of dread.

Let's twist the fabric, pull it tight,
Giggles abound, what a delight!
In this world of thought on a shelf,
I laugh and stitch, just being myself!

Twists of Thought

Thoughts spiral up like a slinky toy,
Every tumble brings a sprinkle of joy.
Round and round, I mix and blend,
A jumble of humor with no end.

Twisting words from here to there,
Creating chaos beyond compare.
A funny slip, a cheeky pun,
In this mental dance, we all have fun.

I tie my brain in silly knots,
A chuckle blooms in wacky spots.
A backward glance, a cartwheel spin,
In the circus of thoughts, let's dive in!

So grab a thread, don't be shy,
Join the fun as we reach for the sky.
For in every twist, in every chance,
Lies a giggle in life's silly dance!

Delicate Tangles

A spider spins a web of laughs,
Each strand a quirky, funny gaffe.
Twisted fibers, bright and wild,
In this mess, I'm still a child.

With delicate tangles, I navigate,
Through the whims of an absurd fate.
Knots of giggles, loops of cheer,
In this mix, I have no fear.

Tangles point in every direction,
Bringing forth unexpected affection.
A twist, a turn, a snicker or two,
In this jumble, I lean into you.

So let's embrace the twisted thread,
With laughter bubbling, it's our stead.
For in every knot, every zany bind,
We find the fun that life designed!

Fabricated Fantasies

In a world where socks just do ballet,
And spoons take tea with bright bouquet.
The cats wear crowns and giggle loud,
As mice in pants dance, feeling proud.

The clouds wiggle like jelly on toast,
While ants write novels, to say the least.
Each bubble pops with a silly sound,
In this land of dreams where laughs abound.

The hedgehogs wear glasses, read the news,
While octopuses juggle in fancy shoes.
And when the sun winks with a cheesy grin,
The joy of the day is where we begin.

So come join the fun, let your wiggles free,
In a land of laughter, just you and me.
Where nonsense reigns and logic takes flight,
In fabricated dreams, everything feels right.

Intricate Echoes

In a forest where the trees gossip and chatter,
The squirrels argue over which branch is better.
While mushrooms debate with the dancing bees,
About the best way to tease the tall trees.

Echoes bounce like rubber, back to the start,
As frogs recite poetry, each with their art.
And owls wear tuxedos, ready to dance,
Singing sweet sonnets with each fleeting glance.

The crickets wear top hats, playing their tunes,
While fireflies twinkle, lighting like moons.
The laughter transforms into echoes profound,
In a rhythm of joy, where fun can be found.

Join the frolic of the curious night,
Where giggles and whispers create pure delight.
In a world where puzzles are all made of sound,
With intricate echoes, new joys abound.

The Threads of Insight

See the wisdom woven in a wise caterpillar,
Who spins tales on threads, making giggles spill-er.
Each stitch is a story, a tale woven tight,
With a needle that dances, oh what a sight!

The spiders are artists with webs made of gold,
While beetles tell secrets, both funny and bold.
And clouds hold meetings, discussing the rain,
In a tapestry of laughter, nothing's mundane.

Jumping from thread to thread, life's a delight,
As humor unravels from morning till night.
With a wink and a nod, insights unfold,
In the fabric of nonsense, stories retold.

So wrap yourself snug in this fabric of fun,
Where wisdom is sprinkled like rays of the sun.
The threads that connect us, all shimmer and shine,
In the dance of insight, where humor's divine.

Interwoven Intentions

In a place where intentions twirl like a dance,
And questions hop about, given the chance.
Where the dogs wear glasses and read the news,
While cats play chess in their shiny shoes.

The goldfish recite the tales of the day,
With bubbles that giggle, in a bubbly way.
And lizards play pranks, with a cheeky grace,
Giving everyone there a smile on their face.

As jumbled thoughts spin round in delight,
Like shoelaces tangled, just out of sight.
Each intention a thread, pulled tight with a grin,
In a tapestry woven where fun can begin.

Dance with the colors, let laughter ignite,
In interwoven dreams that feel just right.
Where the silliness shines and the joy is sincere,
In this vibrant world, let's shout "Hooray!" and cheer!

Mindful Embellishments

Twirling thoughts like candy swirls,
Bouncing ideas, like happy squirrels.
A sprinkle here, a twisty line,
Creating chaos, oh so fine!

Mismatched socks on a sunny day,
A jumble of giggles, come what may.
Jellybeans and paper clips,
Crafting nonsense with happy quips!

An artful mess, a curious sight,
Paddling boats in the moonlight.
With laughter echoing through the air,
Plucking dreams from everywhere!

So dance along this playful spree,
Where nothing's quite as it should be.
In this circus of thoughts we dive,
And paint our world to feel alive!

Fragments of a Daydream

Dancing ducks in top hats gleam,
Waltzing past on a chocolate stream.
Clouds are made of candy floss,
In this realm, we're always boss!

Whimsical thoughts like flying kites,
Chasing shadows under glittering lights.
Bursting bubbles with silly names,
In this madness, nothing's the same!

A teapot full of giggles brews,
Pouring laughter, mixing hues.
Catching whispers on a breeze,
Tickling dreams with playful ease!

In fragments bright, we weave our tale,
A carousel dance with wink and wail.
So grab a friend and join the ride,
In daydreams lost, we'll abide!

The Soft Touch of Enigma

A riddle wrapped in cotton candy,
What's the sound of a ghost that's dandy?
Tickling brains with quirks galore,
Mysteries knock on a playful door!

A whispering cat with merry tales,
Sipping tea in the land of snails.
Jumping jacks from every corner,
Twisting logic like a joyful mourner!

What's the color of a giggle?
A puzzle that makes your brain wiggle.
In this realm of nonsense fun,
Every answer just a pun!

So come parade with puzzled friends,
In a world where logic bends.
With every chuckle, let's explore,
The soft touch of wonder and more!

The Stitches of Perception

Crafting quirks with needle and thread,
Sewing stories in the back of my head.
A patchwork quilt of thoughts so wild,
A playful dance, a curious child!

Snippets of laughter, they tickle the air,
A tapestry woven with giddy flair.
Jigsaw pieces scattered 'round,
In this madcap world, joy is found!

Plucking thoughts like daisies bright,
Stitching dreams in the glowing light.
With every tug, a grin appears,
Embroidery of giggles, melting fears!

So let's embrace this quirky art,
In the fabric of life, let's play our part.
With stitches of joy through every seam,
Together we weave the perfect dream!

A Tapestry of Echoes

In my head, a jumbled thread,
Of silly thoughts and dreams widespread.
A sock that dances, a shoe that sings,
Life's weirdity in a tapestry brings.

Each echo laughs, a chorus loud,
In a sea of giggles, I am proud.
A cat in a hat, what a strange sight,
Dreams weave joy, like day turns to night.

That cookie jar with a life of its own,
Whispers snacks when I'm alone.
Jellybeans dance in a clever parade,
As my mind builds a sweet escapade.

Amidst these threads, I can't resist,
Laughing out loud at this funny twist.
My imagination, a playful friend,
Crafting humor that will never end.

Woven Silhouettes

Shadows prance on the walls, oh dear,
Is that a ghost or just my fear?
A frame of giggles, a wall of cheer,
Woven silhouettes that disappear.

A toaster pops with a jaunty dance,
And toast takes off in a silly prance.
The fridge starts humming a soothing tune,
As I try to make a sandwich that's gone too soon.

Balloons float by with a sassy grin,
Each one telling a joke from within.
A party in here, let's not be shy,
Even the cat wants to try and fly.

So silly are these shapes I weave,
In this world of laughter, I believe.
Every outline, a moment so bright,
Creating joy in the shimmering night.

Patterns of Perception

In a world of quirks and odd designs,
A chicken walks in a line of signs.
It clucks in tune with the beat of the day,
Patterns of perception, come out and play!

A squirrel in shorts with a wild flair,
Doing the cha-cha without a care.
The trees giggle softly in the breeze,
As ants in top hats march with ease.

Cucumbers wearing sneakers parade around,
While jellyfish jive with a slippery sound.
A kaleidoscope of quirky dreams,
Where nothing is ever as it seems.

So join the fun, don't be reserved,
In this silly world, you'll get served.
Every twist and turn brings a smile,
Let's pattern our laughter, stay for a while!

The Fabric of Daydreams

Quilted thoughts of clouds and ice cream,
In the shop of wonders, I pick a theme.
Buttons for noses on dancing bears,
Stitching together the world with flair.

Bubbles of laughter float in the air,
Each one's a whimsy, a giggly affair.
A rainbow that tickles, a rainbow that sings,
In the fabric of daydreams, anything springs.

Tigers in tutus, a picturesque sight,
Waltzing through gardens, pure delight.
The sun wears sunglasses, looking divine,
As I sip my lemonade, feeling fine.

So toss on your fabric, let's craft away,
In this merry realm where we can play.
With every weave, a chuckle to share,
Creating a tapestry beyond compare.

Tangles in the Twilight

In twilight's glow, thoughts twist and twine,
Chasing shadows, sipping on sunshine.
A rogue idea takes a playful leap,
Tickling the brain, making giggles creep.

With every giggle, a thought goes awry,
An idea flutters, then bids goodbye.
Like spaghetti in a bowl, so tangled and bright,
Minds weave together, a silly delight.

Frolicking notions race across the sky,
As truths do somersaults, oh my, oh my!
The jester within grins ear to ear,
While nonsense dances, bringing good cheer.

In this puzzling maze, we stumble in glee,
Finding the joke was all just in me.
So twirl in the twilight, where thoughts intertwine,
In a world made of giggles, everything's fine.

Delicate Patterns of Memory

Memory weaves a tapestry, so fine,
Where moments collide, like sweet lemon-lime.
Doodles of yesteryears tickle the brain,
Each wrinkle of thought is a knot in the chain.

A dream of a pickle in a polka dot dress,
Makes me wonder if I'm under some stress.
Thoughts are a jigsaw, none fit quite right,
Yet I laugh 'til I wheeze, oh what a sight!

Patterns emerge like misfit sock pairs,
With stories that wiggle and wiggle with flares.
Each patch a reminder of laughter or cheer,
In the quilt of my brain, they all feel so near.

A funny old memory, tickled with zest,
Knocks on my thoughts, a haunting jest.
In this carnival of minds, all is a game,
Where every slip of the tongue earns you fame.

Fabric of Dreams

In the fabric of dreams, where silliness flows,
I stitch up the clouds with my whimsical prose.
A quilt made of giggles, a patchwork of joy,
Every seam a memory, a delightful ploy.

I once dreamed of fish who could dance on the moon,
Sipping on stardust, swaying to a tune.
They wore tiny hats, each one a delight,
Inviting me in for a whimsical flight.

Threads of bright colors, each one a tale,
Of penguins on roller skates, off they sail!
They jive through the stars with a wink and a spin,
In this dream of a world where the laughter begins.

So wrap me in fun, let the laughter take thread,
As I drift through the night, with smiles in my head.
In this soft tapestry woven with glee,
May I always explore what the mind dares to see.

Fragile Connections

Connections so fragile, they shimmer and sway,
Like bubbles of laughter that float far away.
A wink from a friend sends the giggles aflame,
Turning seriousness into a playful game.

Thoughts bounce like balls, with a humorous thud,
While honesty dances in a puddle of mud.
Each shared little secret, a thread we can pull,
In the tapestry woven, we play it so cool.

Fragile as whispers, but bold in their cheer,
These links of our laughter are why we stay near.
They sparkle in daylight, and shimmer at night,
Drawing us closer, like magnets of light.

So let's twine our fancies with ribbons of jest,
And cherish connections that make us the best.
In a world filled with humor, we'll giggle and dance,
Embracing our quirks, in this curious chance.

Filigree of Feelings

Tiny thoughts swirl round my head,
Like a cat that's searching for bread.
Ideas tangled in funny knots,
Tickling my brain, tying silly spots.

Giggling whispers, like a breeze,
Fluffy clouds that wander with ease.
I trip over chuckles, they're trapped in air,
Making sense of nonsense, oh what a flair!

Jokes loop like ribbons, they twist and twine,
Each stitch a punchline, a joke divine.
In this patchwork of giggles, I gladly reside,
Worn with a smile, hearts open wide.

Bubbly thoughts dance a silly waltz,
Poking fun at all of life's faults.
With every twist, I find the cheer,
Stitched in laughter, bright and clear.

The Subtle Stitches of Yesterday

Memories float on a whimsy breeze,
Like past adventures in mismatched shoes.
Uneven stitching on tales we've told,
Ties that may fray but are never too old.

A yarn of laughter, a needle of cheer,
Sewing together what once brought fear.
Funny mishaps that tangled our days,
Now shine like jewels in a jester's maze.

With wit that winks and wiggles about,
We celebrate moments, lost but not out.
Threading the needle with humor anew,
Knitting our stories with every hue.

Though time may prickle with sharp little pins,
We stitch up our days with giggles and grins.
In yesterday's closet, we find our threads,
Crafting tomorrow with laughter instead.

Woven Whispers of the Heart

Whispers dance in ticklish loops,
As giddy giggles shape the droops.
Silly secrets woven with care,
Tales of mischief that float in the air.

Every stitch a hearty laugh,
Frayed edges remind us of the gaffe.
Threading smiles in colors bright,
Laughter wraps around, holding tight.

In the fabric of friendships deep,
We share our secrets, our joy to keep.
The hum of jokes fills the room,
Blooming bright, dispelling gloom.

A patchwork quilt of hearty cheer,
Each piece stitched with love and dear.
We craft our stories, one by one,
With woven whispers, oh so fun!

The Delicate Dance of Thoughts

Thoughts pirouette in a grand ballet,
Leaping and spinning in a humorous way.
Each leap is a joke, each turn a laugh,
Chasing the silliness, we find the path.

Waltzing through ideas, we twirl and sway,
Tickling our brains like a playful play.
Words feign a slip and trip in delight,
Launching us high like kites in flight.

With fragile threads in laughter we weave,
A tapestry bright, just hard to believe.
Each giggle a note, sweet music to hear,
As thoughts do the tango, drawing us near.

In this delicate dance, we'll never retreat,
For humor is life, oh what a treat!
So here's to the movement, the fun in the mind,
In the dance of our thoughts, joy's a rare find.

Patterns of Perception

I saw a cat wear shoes, oh what a sight,
Dancing under the moon, feeling just right.
It twisted and turned with such flair,
Inviting all dogs to join with a stare.

The squirrels held a meeting in the big oak tree,
Discussing world domination over green peas.
My mind started spinning like a top in a whirl,
As peanut butter dreams began to unfurl.

A teapot started singing a jazzy tune,
While spoons dipped and dived, oh what a boon!
I laughed so hard, nearly fell off my chair,
Wishing my thoughts could dance like that pair.

With marshmallow clouds and chocolate rain,
The world turned silly, embracing the plain.
Each giggle echoed like a vibrant sound,
In the realm where oddities are truly profound.

Tapestry of Dreams

A pickle in a tux, so sharply dressed,
Took Mr. Tomato to a vine-dancing fest.
They twirled and they whirled, what a visual treat,
A veggie ballet, sure to be beat!

The spoons were a band, with forks as the crowd,
While plates cheered louder, oh my, they were proud!
I raised my glass of soda, a toast to the fun,
To dreams woven richly, like threads in the sun.

Clouds wore pajamas, drifting like glee,
Sharing bedtime stories with the sleepy bee.
With a giggle and a wiggle, all snoozed away,
In a whacky world, where night follows day.

Monkeys with top hats juggling weird fruit,
While walking on tightropes in a big, fancy suit.
I tossed in a laugh as they fell and they spun,
Creating a circus of joy, full of pun!

The Fabric of Imagination

A dandelion dressed like a disco ball,
Flashed colors of joy to one and all.
As bees buzzed loudly, with moves so divine,
They grooved to the rhythm, sipping sweet wine.

The frogs threw a party, with hats piled high,
Underneath the bright stars, they leaped to the sky.
With music so catchy, I caught the tune,
And danced through the dreams of a big, fluffy moon.

Lemons in tutus skipped down the lane,
While oranges played tag, oh what a gain!
The fruit bowl erupted with laughter so bright,
Creating a mix of pure, silly delight.

I slipped on a banana, fell flat on the grass,
As laughter erupted—oh, what a brass!
In the fabric of dreams, where giggles never cease,
I found the seams of joy, a beautiful piece.

Delicate Designs of Desire

A snail in a cape, full of proud delight,
Dreamed of racing a rabbit, oh what a sight!
With winks and a nudge, they both took their chance,
Living life large in a whimsical dance.

Balloons floated by, wearing tiny hats,
Chasing after rainbows, making friends with bats.
They rolled up their strings and painted the sky,
With laughter that twinkled, as if to comply.

A cupcake held court in a world made of pies,
Sipping on cocoa, under chocolate skies.
Each frosting swirl told a story unique,
Of sugar-coated dreams and the fun that we seek.

When jellybeans bounced and sprinkles took flight,
A carnival erupted, a festival bright.
In delicate designs, where joy finds its way,
Life's tasty creations, let's dance and not sway!

Threads of Thought

In the attic of ideas, I found a stray sock,
It danced with old memories, tickled my clock.
Spaghetti of stories, all tangled and wild,
Time to unravel, oh what a child!

A sandwich of nonsense, piled high with glee,
Twirled around jokes that won't let me be.
A pinwheel of laughter spins round in my head,
Chasing the thoughts like a cat on a thread.

Silly old musings, they wobble and sway,
Like jelly on Sunday, they giggle and play.
A circus of giggles with elephants prancing,
Each thought a balloon, oh, they're all romancing!

So here's to the mind, a wonderful show,
With clowns in the back row, putting on a glow.
Let's tether our silliness, let it unwind,
A festival's worth of the threads intertwined.

Weaving Whispers

A whisper of whimsy, soft as a breeze,
Twists through my thoughts, a taste of the cheese.
A hat made of giggles, perched on a hat rack,
Spinning and twirling, there's no looking back.

The invisible loom hums a curious tune,
As shadows of humor dance 'neath the moon.
A tapestry funny, with stitches askew,
Where socks have opinions and cats tell what's true.

Threads of good fortune all tangled in knots,
Like cereal and milk in a mishap of pots.
Weaving together the joys and the woes,
In the fabric of laughter, anything goes!

So gather the snippets, the jokes and the puns,
We'll craft a fine quilt of life's little runs.
With every wild stitch, a new story unfolds,
Oh, what fun it is, in this world full of gold!

Knots of Reflection

Tangled in thoughts like shoelaces now,
Knotting up wisdom, I take a big bow.
Reflections like mirrors, all funny and bright,
Both sides of the story share giggles at night.

A jester's cap giggles, tied in a fuss,
With puns that bounce back like a happy plus.
Threads of confusion all dance with delight,
Making mishaps feel like magic at night.

In a whirl of confusion, the answer is clear,
Just laugh at the madness, give worries a sneer.
Twirls of absurdity, no right or wrong here,
Knotting reflection, oh what a cheer!

So here's to the chaos, the silly, the sweet,
The hilarious journey of dancing on feet.
With threads of connection tying laughter and thought,
Let's revel in knotted reflections we've caught.

Intricate Pathways

Through pathways of giggles, I skip and I twirl,
Each corner a joke, like a flag in a whirl.
A maze full of laughter, not lost but found,
I giggle at echoes that bounce all around.

With each twist and turn, I tumble in grace,
Chasing the humor, a playful embrace.
Like ducks in a row, they waddle and rhyme,
The punchlines parade in a line so sublime.

A map made of chuckles, instructions unclear,
A detour for banter, I steer with a cheer.
Frolicking freely, no speed limit sign,
In intricate pathways, life's humor's divine!

So follow the giggles, in circles we go,
Through tunnels of wit, watch the laughter flow.
Let's wander forever, with joy as our guide,
In this maze of bright moments, come laughter, let's ride!

Intricate Patterns of Emotion

In a dance of thoughts that twirl and spin,
It's like a catwalk where chaos begins.
Juggling giggles while riding a bike,
Logic slips off, oh, what a hike!

Colors clash in a haphazard way,
Twirling umbrellas caught in a fray.
Heart's a jester with tricks in its sleeves,
Who knew feelings were made from leaves?

Each pulse a riddle, wrapped in a bow,
Like trying to catch a slippery glow.
Thoughts play hopscotch in bubblegum dreams,
Where nothing is quite as it seems!

Oh, the brain's a circus of clowns and balloons,
Tickling senses in whimsical tunes.
When logic retreats, laughter will bind,
In this carnival of the mind!

Ties that Bind the Soul

Threading the needle with laughter and cheer,
Stitching together all that we hold dear.
A quirky quilt made of mismatched hues,
Woven tight with giggles, not a single bruise.

Knots of friendship entwined in the air,
Like spaghetti noodles causing a scare.
When thoughts get tangled, just whistle a tune,
And watch worries dance like a balloon!

Each tie's a story, spun from delight,
Sailing on breezes, taking flight.
A tapestry woven with silliness grand,
In this web of joy, together we stand!

So, let's celebrate the quirks and the qualms,
In our patchwork of laughter, nothing calms.
With each knot we tie, a smile we gain,
In the tapestry's chaos, we'll dance in the rain!

Mysteries of the Mind's Canvas

A canvas splattered with whimsical glee,
Painting our thoughts like a twisted marquee.
Imagine pink llamas adorned in a hat,
Just the right touch for a chat with a cat!

Swirls of confusion, bright polka dot skies,
Where logic takes naps while the clown car flies.
Funny little doodles that jump from the page,
Wiggling their toes like they're on a stage!

Balloons of ideas float high in the breeze,
Tickling the senses like late summer tease.
Every stroke giggles, every splash sings,
Making us ponder the silliest things!

So here's to the canvas, a bizarre delight,
Whirling in colors that tickle our sight.
In the puzzle of laughter, our joy will parade,
As we dance through the chaos that whimsically played!

Filaments of Fantasy

Spinning wild tales that sparkle and pop,
Like a merry-go-round that just won't stop.
With unicorns trotting on marshmallow clouds,
And cupcakes laughing in giggly crowds!

A jigsaw of dreams with pieces askew,
Where dragons have tea and fairies play do.
Each twist is a tickle, every turn a tease,
As fantasy dances with whimsical ease!

Threads of imagination weave round and round,
Creating a tapestry of laughter profound.
Can't catch a glimpse of what's real or not,
In this filmy world, all worries are caught!

So let's twirl this filament, bright and tight,
Jump into wonder, take flight, take flight!
In this zany carousel of bright fantasy,
Every misstep is just part of the spree!

Patterns of Perception

A squirrel in a suit, oh what a sight,
Chasing his own tail, with all his might.
Hats made of fruit, they wobble and sway,
In this silly dreamland, we dance and play.

Fish ride bicycles, they honk as they go,
Waving to turtles, just stealing the show.
Umbrellas like poppies rain down from the sky,
While elephants giggle, they flip and fly.

The map of our thoughts has a colorful maze,
With paths made of candy, and wild, greedy gaze.
Jellybeans serve as the currency here,
You chuckle and trade for your favorite cheer.

Through quirky designs we tiptoe and twirl,
In this technical fabric, we spin and whirl.
Each pattern a whisper, a laugh and a jest,
In this loop of reflections, we're all quite blessed.

Elysian Threads

Imagine a world woven wild and bright,
Where socks attend parties and dance through the night.
With unicorns prancing in pajamas of gold,
And jellyfish swirling in stories retold.

Magic teapots sing whilst spinning their tales,
With cupcakes that sail and with candy canails.
The rain is confetti, it sprinkles with cheer,
As each joyful moment draws everyone near.

Walking on sunshine with shoes made of dreams,
You trip over rainbows, or so it seems.
Hiccups bring giggles, the humor is pure,
In this land of delight, you'll always find more.

The laughter's infectious, like music so sweet,
We dance with the clouds while we twirl on our feet.
In threads of elation, our hearts intertwine,
A tapestry vivid, your joy meets with mine.

Braided Fantasies

In a garden of wishes, where wishes take flight,
Lollipops grow tall, oh, what a delight!
Pirates in pajamas sail clouds made of fluff,
While kittens play poker, they've really got bluff!

Comets play tag in the shimmering blue,
While llamas in capes shout, "We're coming for you!"
Balloons filled with giggles float high in the air,
And the wind tells the secrets that only we share.

A bicycle built for two rides the breeze,
As giggling fairies dodge ears made of cheese.
The stakes are all jelly, the table's a dream,
In this curious land, nothing's as it seems.

With ribbons of laughter, we braid our own fate,
As we bounce on the clouds, oh, isn't it great?
In fantasies woven with whimsical threads,
Our hearts are the colors our laughter spreads.

Shadows of Stitchery

In shadows of whimsy, we stitch up the fun,
With tortoises pro-wrestling under the sun.
Each patch tells a story, absurd and absurder,
Where spaghetti gets tangled in each silly letter.

Bouncing balloons whisper the secrets of night,
While owls wear top hats and giggle in flight.
A circus of crickets performs for the moon,
As polka-dots dance to their own merry tune.

Join the parade of mismatched delight,
With sandals on penguins and bears in plight.
Each quirk has a tale that tickles the mind,
With stitches of laughter, our joy intertwined.

The fabric of nonsense wraps tight around glee,
In shadows of stitchery, come dance with me!
For humor is woven in all that we see,
In this dance of absurdity, wild and free.

Entangled Echoes

In a tangle of thoughts, I sit and stare,
My brain's like a puzzle, nowhere to spare.
Ideas like socks, mismatched and bright,
Dance on the edges, delight in the night.

Whispers of nonsense twirl in my ears,
Tickling my ribs and igniting my fears.
Bananas in pajamas are plotting a scheme,
While jellybeans argue in a sugar-crazed dream.

A feathery thought floats, then suddenly bounces,
Like a frog on a trampoline, laughter announces.
The echo of chuckles cascades all around,
As my mind juggles galas where nonsense is found.

Oh, the chaos of humor, so twisted and loud,
From the circus of neurons, I'm ever so proud.
With giggles and quirks, I'll dance on the line,
In this carnival of thoughts, how splendidly mine!

Twisting Pathways of Perception

Wandering pathways where logic caves in,
My thoughts are a circus, let the madness begin!
A rhino wearing glasses rides a big wheel,
While penguins on bicycles make quite the appeal.

The signposts are silly, the roads often twist,
Where squirrels hold meetings, and giggles persist.
A traffic jam puzzles made of marshmallow fluff,
Followed by unicorns that simply won't bluff.

Each turn is a riddle, a whimsical jest,
Where laughter erupts with each silly quest.
From the aisle of oddities, I take a small peek,
Finding humor in corners, never feeling weak.

A labyrinth fraught with confetti and cheer,
It tickles the soul, makes the chaos so clear.
So come take a stroll through this mind's wild spree,
Where each twist points to fun, just wait and see!

The Weft of Whimsy

In a quilt of absurdity, I snuggle tight,
With patches of laughter that shimmer and bite.
My thoughts weave in colors, a glorious blend,
Where absurdity wanders but never can end.

A cat in a bow tie is baking a cake,
While elephants juggle with tops made of flakes.
The waltz of the ridiculous flares up my mind,
As a parrot in top hat speaks riddles unkind.

Tangled in wonders, I chase after dreams,
Navigation is tricky, or so it seems.
For each thread I pull leads to giggles anew,
In this tapestry woven with sunshine and dew.

So let's tickle the fibers of fun with delight,
A whimsy parade through the day and the night.
With a nod and a wink, I embrace the design,
In this fabric of laughter, my heart will align!

Threads of the Unconscious

Hidden in shadows, my thoughts twist and dance,
Where dreams sip on pancakes and take a free chance.
A fish wearing sneakers recites Shakespeare's lines,
While cupcakes in sunglasses enjoy sunny shines.

In this realm of weirdness, fun reigns supreme,
I float on a cloud spun from candy and cream.
Ideas are pushed by a breeze made of cheer,
As sock puppets plot, whispering in my ear.

The threads of the strange weave stories so bright,
In colors of giggles and sprinkle-filled light.
Oh, the places my mind goes, such curious sights,
With oddities thriving in fanciful flights.

So here in the swirl of my mind's lively spree,
I'll relish the humor, oh, how it delights me!
For thoughts intertwined bring joy as they spin,
In this circus of whimsy, let the laughter begin!

Patterns in the Ether

In the realm where thoughts entwine,
Ideas dance like vines on twine.
They spin and whirl, a jolly race,
Creating patterns that bring a smile to face.

Nonsense bubbles, laughter flies,
Unexpected truths in clever guise.
Mindful chaos, a jester's play,
Crafting joy in a quirky way.

Dreams adorned with silly hats,
Giggles sprung from curious chats.
Wit stitched in a patchwork quilt,
Fun is born from whims we've built.

So let us frolic, gleeful hearts,
We're all artists with our funny parts.
In this ether, our thoughts take flight,
A carnival of shapes, a pure delight.

Filigree of Emotion

Woven feelings, a quirky thread,
Tickling fancy, dancing ahead.
Joy and goofy grace combine,
Sprightly echoes of a punchline.

Whimsies flicker, like fireflies,
Bright ideas wearing silly ties.
Nostalgic giggles weave a tale,
A carnival where no heart can pale.

In the tapestry of a mind's delight,
The jests and japes take center stage, so bright.
Every thought a playful stroke,
Creating mischief with every poke.

Amidst the chaos, colors clash,
Comedic sparks in a vibrant splash.
Here we frolic, no fear to find,
A frenzy of art in the tangled mind.

Entangled Reveries

In dreams where quirks and giggles bloom,
Thoughts sprout legs and dance around the room.
Loopy patterns, a thread of jest,
Wrap around the mind like a cozy nest.

Silly ponderings float like balloons,
Round and round in wacky tunes.
They tumble, twirl, and never end,
Turning moments into a playful blend.

Imagination, a furry cat,
Pouncing on ideas, imagine that!
Each notion caught, a playful chase,
Bringing laughter to each space.

So let's get lost in whimsy's weave,
Silly treasures we dare to believe.
Life's a chatty, giggly friend,
In entangled dreams, let fun transcend.

A Mosaic of Musings

Bits of laughter, colors collide,
Thoughts scatter wide, no need to hide.
Each quirk a tile in this grand design,
Crafting smiles that brightly shine.

Ideas bumble like bees in flight,
Buzzing all day, full of delight.
A mosaic made of whims and play,
Turning serious into a bright bouquet.

Snippets of dreams, playful and odd,
Dance around like a cheeky god.
Creative chaos, a fun parade,
Every notion glimmers like a charade.

So join the mix, let laughter ring,
Celebrate what silly thoughts can bring.
In this vibrant canvas, we shall find,
The joyful patches of a quirky mind.

Threads of Yesterday

In a box, old photos lay,
Worn-out smiles from yesterday.
These threads of time, they twist and twine,
Making me laugh at the absurd design.

Grandpa's hat, it flies like a kite,
Mom's big hair, what a sight!
We danced like fools in mismatched socks,
Caught in the web of memory's locks.

Each thread a story, each loop a cheer,
Why do we laugh when they appear?
Nostalgia's giggle, a silly surprise,
A tapestry made of our alibis.

So let's unwind this playful mess,
Life's a quilt, stitched to impress.
With sprinkles of joy and stitches of glee,
Let's weave a tale, just you and me.

Interlaced Realities

In dreams, I'm a cat with a top hat on,
I juggle my snacks on the front lawn.
Reality spins, it's quite a jest,
Who knew life's a carnival at its best?

Once, I tripped on spaghetti for fun,
Landed on laughter, oh what a run!
With threads of nonsense, I weave through each phase,
Crafting my days in a whimsical maze.

A squirrel debates with a rubber duck,
In this fabric of nonsense, who has bad luck?
We exchange secrets, they chatter with glee,
On this wild ride, nothing's too free.

So tip your hat to the silly and keen,
Life's a patchwork, forever unseen.
With stitches of laughter and colors so bright,
We dance through the mayhem, pure delight.

Weft of the Soul

With every mishap, life weaves its thread,
I slip on a banana, fall flat on my head.
Chuckling and tumbling, I rise once more,
Wondering what else is behind that door.

Got an umbrella that roars like a train,
Opened it once, it just won't close again!
Raindrops run riot, we all scream and shout,
Who knew umbrellas could laugh and pout?

In this fabric of whimsy where laughter ignites,
Woven together, life's bumpy delights.
Each weft a wonder, each spin a cheer,
Is that a clown jumping out of my beer?

So come, let's frolic, let's fumble, and play,
In the tapestry of joy, we'll merrily sway.
With threads of the silly and laughter's embrace,
Weft of our souls, find joy in this space.

The Loom of Imagination

On a loom of dreams, I braid and I spin,
Creating a world, let the fun begin!
A talking toaster sings a tune so sweet,
As dancing waffles, they tap their feet.

Under the table, a sock puppet roars,
Declaring itself king of the kitchen floors.
With every stitch, I craft silly scenes,
Where broccoli wears sunglasses and sips on beans.

Bouncing ideas like popcorn in air,
Every little notion, a vibrant affair.
The fabric of chuckles, the patterns of play,
Imagination's thread keeps boredom at bay!

So grab your yarn and let's knit a jest,
In the loom of wonder, we'll quirkily invest.
With colors so bold and laughter so bright,
We'll weave through the night, till dawn's early light.

Lattice of Longing

In a garden where thoughts twist and twirl,
Dreams can get knotted like a pearl.
Chasing the whims of an old mangy cat,
Finding myself lost in a tall, floppy hat.

Tangled up feelings in a bright red string,
Giggling at nonsense, oh, what joy it can bring!
Whispers of wishes dance in a breeze,
Like silly balloons, floating with ease.

Jigsaw of laughter, a puzzle so wide,
Trying to fit it, but I push it aside.
Thoughts play hopscotch on a sunny day,
And here I am, chasing them all the way.

Wandering whimsies, oh where do they roam?
Tying me down while I'm dreaming of home.
In this maze of musings, I sit with a grin,
For the chaos of longing is where I begin.

The Soft Weaving of Reflections

Not a weaver, just pretending to be,
Knitting up smiles as bright as can be.
Fuzzy memories wrapped up in yarn,
Swapping the truth for a bit of charm.

Threads of thought twist in colors so bright,
Dancing around like they're ready for flight.
Frogs in top hats jumping around in a line,
Barcode memories singing a silly design.

Pull on a string and unravel a tale,
Of socks in the fridge, oh what a fail!
Reflective giggles bounce from wall to wall,
As the soft weaving invites us to fall.

Tangled up wonders through laughter they glide,
Bursting with joy, oh how I confide!
Fluttering fancies in patterns of schemes,
Chasing the shadows of whimsical dreams.

Patterns of Perception

Swirling in circles like a wobbly fly,
Perceptions play tricks when I try to comply.
A hat on my head, don't ask how it got there,
Laughter erupts, oh, I just don't care!

Patterns emerge in a baffling hue,
Banana peels slip, and the rubber ducks flew.
Hilarity mounts as I lose my way,
In the funhouse of thoughts where sillies can stay.

Much ado about nothing, it seems ever clear,
When intertwined ideas bring forth a cheer.
Painting the world in a polka-dotted spree,
Funny little fabric of all that we see.

Refracting reality like a clown in the night,
Twisting the mundane, what a curious sight!
In patterns confusing, our laughter we find,
As joy weaves the tapestry tucked in our mind.

The Entangled Maze of Memory

In a maze of giggles where memories play,
Each twist and turn leads the mind a new way.
Chasing a clown with a red rubber nose,
Through this wild ride, the excitement just grows.

Thoughts loop like ribbons, so tangled yet bright,
Leading me deeper into sweet silly nights.
Fuzzy past moments as soft as a cloud,
Laughter erupts; oh, aren't we so proud!

Faces pop up, like balloons in the air,
Fizzing with fun as I trip on a chair.
Chasing the thoughts that dart in and out,
With each silly stumble, joy bursts into shout.

In this entangled maze, I confidently roam,
Finding the funny, I feel right at home.
In twists of recall, where whimsy is key,
Laughter's the thread that weaves you and me.

Remnants of a Dreamscape

In the realm where thoughts collide,
I found a sock that tried to hide.
It spoke in riddles, spun quite around,
As I laughed while lost, in the lost and found.

A teacup danced with a broomstick's grace,
Over clouds of cotton, in a silly race.
The moon wore pajamas, quite out of style,
As dreams played tag, all the while.

A fish in a hat, swimming through air,
Singing the stars with a flamboyant flair.
Tickling the rainbows with socks on their fins,
In this wacky place, where nonsense begins.

So gather your slippers, your daydreams too,
For adventures await when the night's made for two.
With giggles as lanterns, we'll wander and play,
In this dreamscape realm where we'll surely stay.

Patterns of a Hidden Journey

Upon the map, a donut appears,
Marked 'Danger Zone' with sprinkles and cheers.
A penguin in boots led us astray,
On a cake-shaped ship, churning all day.

We laughed with a cactus, it tickled us pink,
As we sailed through syrup, just stopping to blink.
The compass spun wildly, a clock with no hands,
As we danced through the jellybean lands.

A mushroom conductor sang 'Don't Be Upset!'
To the rhythm of giggles, we'd never forget.
Floating on marshmallows, we soared through the skies,
Dodging all troubles that wanted a rise.

So pack all your nonsense in one tiny sack,
Join in the revelry, never look back.
For every odd journey holds stories untold,
Where laughter's the treasure, and joy's worth its gold.

Threads of Thought

In a fabric shop filled with odd little thoughts,
I found bits of giggles and whimsical knots.
A turtle in glasses, said, 'Take your time!'
As we knitted together, our words turned to rhyme.

Threads of spaghetti, tangled in plight,
Broke into laughter, twinkling with light.
A hammock of snickers, swung over our heads,
While balloons shaped like poodles danced on our beds.

We stitched up a dream with a needle of fun,
As the clock ticked backwards, we'd just begun.
With pockets of sunshine, we threaded the day,
In a world spun from joy, where the weirdness holds sway.

So gather your buttons, your frays, and your tears,
Let's craft a fatigued smile that conquers our fears.
With threads that connect every whimsical part,
Together we weave this curious art.

Weaving Whispers

In the quiet of whispers, the secrets unfold,
A squirrel spun yarn from the stories they told.
With a wink and a giggle, they stitched up a tale,
Of a fish in a suit who set off to sail.

Through fields of wild giggles, we twirled round and round,
In a garden of quirk, where oddities abound.
A cupcake with wheels rolled by the green beans,
As daisies told jokes with their silly routines.

Hold tight to the flutter of whimsical breezes,
As we craft funny dreams in the land where it sneezes.
With whispers of wonder and chuckles that bind,
Weaving through laughter, the threads that we find.

So dance with the shadows that flip-flop and swoon,
In a world stitched together by silly cartoons.
For every bright whisper, a joy to befriend,
In this tapestry fun, where laughter won't end.

Tapestry of Echoes

In the attic where the squirrels play,
Memories spin in disarray.
A tangle of thoughts just like a cake,
Baking confusion, oh, what a mistake!

Echoes bounce off the wall so sweet,
Dancing round on tiny feet.
They trip and giggle, causing a fuss,
In the fabric room, they are quite a plus!

Whispers slide through the cozy seams,
Woven wonders and silly dreams.
Knitting nonsense, one stitch at a time,
The laughter weaves, oh, what a rhyme!

So when you ponder, don't be shy,
Just tie it up with a goofy tie.
For in the weave of thoughts so bright,
The most absurd can bring delight!

Textures of the Mind

Sketching thoughts in funky lines,
Twirling visions in crafty designs.
A splash of colors that never match,
Bridges crossing, oh! Let's detach!

Patterns float like balloons in rain,
Bouncing around, causing some pain.
A patchwork quilt of giggles and grins,
The art of chaos, where everyone wins!

Tickles and twirls, ideas collide,
In this crazy patch, we take a ride.
Textures tangle, like hair gone wild,
Each strand a treasure, so lovingly piled!

So sift through layers, find the surprise,
A plushy idea that flies and flies.
In the realm of thought, let's not be blind,
Embrace the funny, leave doubt behind!

The Whispers Between Threads

In the sewing box, where secrets hide,
Poking and prodding, giggles nationwide.
Threads like snakes, they twist and shout,
Creating riddles, oh what a rout!

They whisper jokes, so light and spry,
Wiggling softly as they weave and die.
Each little fiber has tales to tell,
Of clumsy dances and triumphs to yell!

Between the stitches, mischief brews,
Spinning yarns of silly views.
A knot of hilarity, tied up neat,
Together in laughter, we're quite the feat!

So come along, let's spin and twine,
Creating memories sweet like wine.
In the fabric of fun, let's all unwind,
With whispers of laughter, we're perfectly aligned!

Netting the Infinite

Casting nets of puzzling thought,
Catching ideas—oh, what a lot!
With holes so big, a fish could flee,
But we catch giggles, just you and me!

Each loop and twist, a talespin ride,
Entangled minds, let's not divide.
In this net, we find the stream,
That leads us on a zigzag dream!

So throw your nets into the sky,
Catch shimmering thoughts that float on by.
We'll haul in chuckles, the bigger the bait,
The more we gather, just wait, don't be late!

In an ocean of whimsy, we'll swim and glide,
With nets of laughter, our hearts open wide.
Come dive with me into this dance,
For in the silly depths, we find our chance!

Stitches of Serenity

In the quiet corner, thoughts unwind,
Threading giggles, oh what a find!
Mystic patches on a canvas bright,
Sewing smiles in the morning light.

Every whimsy tangled with delight,
Whiskers of dreams take joyous flight.
Each loop and knot a playful tease,
Crafting chaos with effortless ease.

Quirky patterns in a soft embrace,
Woven wit in this silly space.
Tickles of laughter, ready to spin,
Stitches of joy where troubles begin.

A needle dances, oh what a show,
On this fabric of thoughts, we all know.
Threads of the heart twist and twine,
Creating a quilt of the absurd divine.

Entangled in Reverie

In the tapestry of a sleepy dream,
I find myself caught in a whimsical stream.
Jumbled thoughts like butterflies free,
Flapping wildly, come join the spree!

Cotton candy clouds, oh what a sight,
Floating through giggles, pure delight.
Overgrown gardens of silly ideas,
Tickling my fancy, igniting my cheers.

A tangled yarn of bright, bold hues,
Each twist and turn brings colorful views.
Lost in the maze of laughter and cheer,
Every zany thought pulls me near.

Threads of whimsy stitch up my soul,
Creating a quilt that makes me whole.
With every knot, joy's bright design,
I'm all tangled up, but oh, that's just fine!

Frayed Edges of Memory

Memories flutter with messy delight,
Capers and blunders stitched up tight.
Frayed edges dance in a whimsical breeze,
Reminding me of silliness that never flees.

Patches of laughter, some worn and torn,
Stories arise from the rags reborn.
Silly missteps tied with a bow,
Frayed edges gleaming, a funny show!

Fabric of folly, so brightly it shone,
With every giggle, we're never alone.
Memories woven with threads of delight,
Frayed edges sparkle, lighting the night.

In the sewing room, chaos is king,
Every mishap becomes a zing.
Rugged rags of the past entwine,
Turning old laughs into a grand design.

The Net of Nostalgia

In the net of the past, I find my prey,
Catching chuckles from yesterday.
Snagged in the web of whimsical schemes,
Tangled in threads of delightful dreams.

Giggles caught like fish in a pond,
Reeling in memories, oh, I'm so fond!
Netting moments, bright as the sun,
Every retrieval, a licensed fun.

With each silly catch, I dance and sway,
Casting my thoughts in a playful way.
Nostalgia's net is woven with glee,
Trapping the moments that set me free.

A playful pull on my heartstrings tight,
Each snicker and snort, my pure delight.
In the net of whimsy, forever I'll stay,
Revisiting laughter, come what may.

Silken Paths of Memory

A thread unwinds in giggles bright,
Twisting tales by day and night.
Forgotten socks and dances strange,
All tied up in a mental range.

Mind's a place where marbles roll,
Chasing thoughts like a cheeky shoal.
Silly visions, a squirrel's race,
Bouncing ideas in a wacky space.

Clumsy curls of daydream fun,
Looping puzzles, one by one.
Knotted words that make us grin,
A playful twist, where laughs begin.

With every twist, a chuckle shared,
Inside our heads, a circus bared.
Fun and folly, they intertwine,
In silly patterns, perfectly fine.

Fragments of the Soul

Bits of laughter tucked away,
In pockets where we love to play.
A hiccup here, a snort or two,
Each little piece a snapshot true.

Glimmers of joy, like shiny beads,
Strung together, where humor feeds.
Whimsical whispers float and weave,
In a tapestry we can't believe.

Our brains a jigsaw, odd and bright,
Missing pieces, yet feeling right.
Quirky shapes that start to dance,
Just one old joke can start a prance.

Silly fragments flit and fly,
Like fireflies in the evening sky.
Together they form a giggle song,
Where all the weird bits truly belong.

A Mosaic of Thoughts

Tiles of memories, bright and odd,
Crafting stories, giving a nod.
Puns and giggles, chaos unfolds,
In a silly quilt where laughter molds.

Swirls of nonsense, colors explode,
Stitching moments, we share the load.
Laughing echoes, patterns collide,
A mosaic of quirks where we can't hide.

Each little chip tells a tale,
Of goofy dreams where we set sail.
With quirks like glue, they stick around,
In playful chaos, joy is found.

Life's a puzzle of jest in place,
Filled with humor, endless grace.
With each odd piece, we share the time,
A canvas of fun, truly sublime.

The Threads that Bind

Twists and turns of jolly thoughts,
Binding laughter with silly knots.
Jests and jigs that catch the breeze,
Weaving smiles with playful ease.

Clumsy stitches, mischief takes flight,
In the fabric of day and night.
Jokes and giggles, a riotous thread,
A tapestry of fun, brightly spread.

Bouncing off the walls of our mind,
Wacky tales of every kind.
With every loop, connections grow,
In the warmth of humor, we know.

So let us stitch the tales we weave,
In friendship's fabric, we believe.
Where laughter binds, and joy shines bright,
Through silly threads, we find delight.

www.ingramcontent.com/pod-product-compliance
Lightning Source LLC
Chambersburg PA
CBHW060114230426
43661CB00003B/178